C0-AJQ-819

# THE BURNING BUSH

ALSO BY POLLY LASZLO BRODY

*Other Nations* (poems, 1999)

# THE BURNING BUSH

Essays with Poems

by

## Polly Laszlo Brody

**Antrim House**
**Simsbury, Connecticut**

Copyright © 2005 by Polly Laszlo Brody

All rights reserved

Library of Congress Control Number: 2005926083

ISBN 0-9762091-5-2


Printed in the United States of America


First Edition

2005


Cover painting: JoAnn M. Andrews

Photo of author: Phelps Tibor Laszlo


Antrim House
www.antrimhousebooks.com
860.217.0023

# ACKNOWLEDGEMENTS

My heartfelt thanks to Brett Warren, for her wonderfully careful reading of this book's first draft, and her enthusiastic response to the writing. My love and gratitude to Susan Deborah King for her unstinting support of all my work, and for her continuous presence in my life as a wise and beloved spirit sister. Thankful appreciation to my Wood Thrush Poet colleagues for their encouragement as I ventured from poetry into prose, and their patience when I brought these chapters to our workshops.

My thanks also to William T. S. Butler, for teaching me what questions to ask during production of this book.

It has been a pleasure to work with my publisher, Rennie McQuilkin, whose suggestions applied a fine editorial polish to the manuscript, and whose enthusiasm for this book has been most heartening.

I should like to acknowledge the following journals, in which poems contained in this collection first appeared:

*Ball State University Forum:* "February Eagle"
*Embers:* "Takes-His-Eagle"
*Fair Fields:* "Foxing"
*The Spoon River Poetry Review:* "Nurse Logs"

"Nurse Logs" received the Connecticut Poetry Society's Winchell Award.

To my brother, Phelps Tibor Laszlo
and my sister, Ilona Laszlo Higgins—
we three sprung from the same root stock

# THE BURNING BUSH

"...all things are crouched in eagerness to become something else."

—Peter Beagle

# THE BURNING BUSH

# Omphalos

I walk downslope to your darkness
pooled there in the valley's cup,
slip off my chrysalis of clothing
and step into you.
Your cool liquid caresses my ankles,
my calves, behind my knees,
slides over my hips and belly.
I lean forward and lay myself
upon you, glide into you.
Your black silk sweeps along my ribcage,
along my reaching arms, curves in gentle
bow-waves against my breasts.
I swim in cool, black silk.
Moon, rising full, draws her train
upon your onyx surface.
I turn into her wake,
stroke through quicksilver,
light rippling at my throat.
From my palms whirl discs of light.
I roll onto my back,
spread outstretched on you,
eyes closed, fingers lax,
head, back, buttocks, legs
buoyed on your cool depth,
laved in moonlight
and your blackness.

# As the Twig is Bent

My brother and I, alone among the beings in this world, remember in our bones a particular childhood path that wandered through a wood beyond our boundary wall.

An obscure trail, it was embarked upon by way of a massive tangle of catbriar and shrubs, and could not be discerned until one had pressed through the briars. None but my younger brother, myself, and our dogs ever seemed to be present on it.

Before my mind's eye pass recollections that are *felt* rather than seen: the scramble over our stonewall, catch of thorns plucking my jacket and jean-clad legs, winning past this barrier into a woodland leafy and still, winning to ground easy to walk upon. The little path led on: past an impressive ledge to my left, leaf-strewn and seamed with a possibility of copperhead dens; past wagon-sized boulders, relics left by a retreating glacier of the last ice age; farther on, coming to the verge of a secretive, small pond completely enclosed by trees. It was a dark brown eye imbedded in gloaming, holding hints of hidden presence.

From this sylvan pond in April, myriad voices of "spring peepers" shrilled loudly musical when we stood by their water-edge, but were a delicate, entrancing chorus when heard from our bedroom windows, which faced their way. Each spring, my brother and I strove to be the first to hear and announce: *the peepers are singing again!*

Our sister, thirteen years younger, never knew that trail in the wood. By the time she was of age to wander unchaperoned by parent, a housing development had claimed that acreage.

Gone as well was the pair of linked pastures, in which piebald Holsteins once grazed and through whose narrow isthmus the mad mare thundered—her hoofbeats warning of her arrival in the upper pasture where I might be playing. That thudding sent me racing for a hut-sized boulder that sat in the field and was more than once my refuge.

Children of the tract homes knew a different landscape. Pastures became smoothed rectangles of lawn. The deep, dark pupil of our forest pool was opened to the sky, its enclosing grove cut down so that neighborhood families might keep a rowboat or two tethered at pond's edge. Youngsters then dimpled its water with their oars—water declaring fair blue sky and cotton clouds, but no more mysteries.

I do not know if *hylas* still sing there, when April comes.

Years later, bringing up my own two children in a Connecticut countryside, I often took them with me for strolls along Deep Brook Road—a dirt lane barely one mile from our home on Main Street. We followed the seasons there: investigated icicles along the frozen streamlet, listened to songs of springtime birds, watched the hover of swallowtail butterflies, gathered brilliant autumn leaves.

Over the next thirty years, I often walked that road. It is amazing, given contemporary never-stay-put styles, that both the road and I remained in place so long. No tarring crew came to widen and gouge it and pave it over. In the course of three decades, many pros and cons were threshed to clarity in my mind, as feet took me on that familiar way.

Deep Brook Road in June was embowered. Briar roses bloomed over the weathered fencing and stone walls that flanked it, and everywhere gushed cool, sweet perfume. Inside their thorny sanctuary might be a Gray Catbird's nest, perhaps a Song Sparrow's too. What a universe to be fledged in!

One section of road ran through a bit of woodland. Flowering edges gave way to the cool green of Christmas Fern, Solomon's Seal, and the gleaming jade of Catbriar. Here bee-like flies hovered, each holding station at the margin of a sun-splash in the dappled shade. They appeared each June, taking their places at each oasis of light. Tulip Poplars grew along this stretch of road, their trunks tall and straight as masts. They lifted regal crowns above the woodland canopy, and lavishly flowered out of sight aloft. After the blossoms dropped, they lay in scatters of creamy petals, each with its thumbprint of orange, aground within the drip zone of each tree.

Where a vista opened over hay meadows, wild iris marked the hidden brook's bank—their blue flags exotic color in the blonde, ripening grass. In July, the meadow raised assertive stalks of milkweed thrusting above tangles of Lamb's-quarter and flannel-leafed Mullein. The milkweed stems were topped with clenched green nodules that would soon relax and open into flowers. Ladybugs, perched on these green fistlets, shone like flakes of burnt sienna lacquer. In the years before fear of deer ticks and Lyme Disease put it off limits, I would walk into this wild garden and lie down beneath its doily spread of Queen Anne's Lace. There I learned the sky was azure fretwork, seen through that lovely filigree.

My childhood had also thrived in the midst of meadows and woods. Our parents raised three of us in a country home. We were taught how to mow, prune, pull weeds; how to handle a shotgun, .22 rifle, and a two-man saw; how to feed chickens, collect their eggs, and pluck the pullet sacrificed for our dinner table.

Mother read bedtime stories by Thornton W. Burgess: tales of Reddy Fox, Johnny Chuck, Jimmy Skunk and Danny Meadow Mouse. Grandfather Frog dispensed his *chug-a-rum* wisdom from a lily pad on the Smiling Pool. Those animals were vivid beings to me. I drank in the lore of field and forest: names of plants, where and when they flourished. How effort-lessly I learned the relationship between predator and prey—made clear in a non-pejorative fashion. It was not malice that closed Hooty the Owl's talons around Danny Meadow Mouse, but rather inattention on Danny's part. His hairbreadth escape thrilled me. Reddy Fox and Granny Fox may have schemed ways to dine off Peter Rabbit, yet they were only doing what is natural for foxes.

I was on Reddy's side when he fled from Bowser the hound. Many autumn foxes fled through fields adjacent to my home, bayed by the Fairfield County Hounds...

## FOXING

Hounds racket through woods next door,
hot on scent laid behind a streak of rust
trying for den in the meadow,
running with ears turned to
that bedlam of grounded geese.
With those cries come sports
in polished boots, fawn britches
clasping the sides of bay horses.
Hidden behind an ash and our stone wall,
I howl—hurl barks, falsetto yelps,
to intercept this pack.
It hears me. Trail-focused tongues
falter and fall into babble.
Here they come—black, tan and white
foxhounds surround me,
stay as I howl on...

In the forest
an hysterical bugle toots.

I was never found out.

Now a middle-aged adult, lecturing on animal communication, I demonstrate hound baying, along with timber wolf howls, crow caws, and herring gull screeches. It all began with Burgess' Bedtime Stories.

My education nestled deep: following with a wooden rake behind Dad's Gravely mower (that infernal machine), I gathered fresh hay windrows; took turns at the long, two-person saw, swaying in tandem with my father at its other end as pungent sawdust piled below our deepening cut; watched my father throw hefty oak sections into the maw of our great fieldstone hearth when winter came. What a galaxy of sparks flew up!

I recall every cranny of the seven acres in which we lived: the spot where Marsh Marigolds bloomed each April and a bit of quaky bog caught my boots, almost sucking them off when I took a cross-lots short cut home from school; a particular sun-warmed boulder where I'd sit humming, filled with the contentment of a long summer stretching ahead; my mother's rock garden on the slope leading to our front door; the oak sapling we planted on that slope after Roosevelt (President beloved in our household) passed away. Recollections endure.

There is a Hungarian adage (at least Dad claimed it for his people): *as the twig is bent, so grows the tree.* Indeed, I am a country woman.

# BACKWARD GLANCES

Selket, I'm held by your golden face,
your great black eyes and brows,
elegant nostrils,
small closed mouth.
The muscles in your cheek and jaw
are taut.  Your open palms blessed
the young king's viscera
and charged an ancient space
with radiant devotion.

Elongate arms today embrace
the empty air,
his coffin taken from them.
You stand now mounted
on a plastic cube
behind a Lucite screen
muted, as you never were then,
Lady.

Selket is one of the four statuettes that were placed
around the casket containing Tutankhamun's internal
organs.  The goddesses guarded his immortality.  Selket
was removed along with all the other grave goods when

his tomb was emptied. The exquisite beauty of these artifacts drew gasps of admiration (my own included) when they were put on view in New York City. Certainly the craft and sophistication of Egyptian art is marvelous. Yet I felt unsettled by the knowledge that they were brought to us as loot.

Some years ago, I watched a television special depicting the first submersible's arrival at the wreck of the *Titanic*. The vast hulk waited two and a half miles below the surface—as far below in the water column as the highest Rocky Mountain rises above sea level. It lay broken-backed, split fore from aft by the impact when it hit bottom.

Now I-MAX cameras scanned the liner's wrecked body, illuminating it in three cones of light. We saw window rectangles, shutters thrust aside: terrified people had forced themselves through those cabin windows. Sections of deck rail were still intact: over these, desperate hundreds had leaped in their final moments.

A piece of filigreed gold-work shone in the grasp of a metal claw manipulated from the submersible, and moments later the camera focused on a glistening candle sconce. The Russian captain of this expedition said gently: "Nothing will be removed from this resting place."

The claw opened and we watched the sconce tumble back to the sea floor. Its impact raised a billow of dingy orange turbidity.

All the while there had been a slow-motion falling—a ceaseless "snow" of particles drifting down through two and a half liquid miles. These debris motes add themselves to a deep plush nap of detritus that

overlays solid sea bottom. Features of the ship's super-
structure and hull were already softened by a drape of
cohering silt. This shroud, accreting over time, will
blur and finally conceal the titan bedded here. All its
human artifice, both grand and delicate, will become
a simple, gentle mound.

Why does it seem sacrilegious to retrieve artifacts
from this sunken liner, yet for some not an invasion of
sanctuary to remove grave relics of long-ago cultures?
Perhaps because this burial mound embodies recent
tragedy, one that was vividly documented? We still see
those lost souls in our mind's eye because they are
contemporary. Human beings centuries and millennia
before us are wraiths. We may conjure them in our
imagination or "reconstruct" them based on inter-
pretation of their goods and bones, but we do not feel
*responsible* to them.

Incised across a great rock wall in Utah, I once
saw a daisy chain of figures holding hands. The
perspective was such that those triangle torsos with
stick-like arms and legs seemed to dwindle into space
and time. So too, I felt, do real identities—individual
beings—recede into the mystery of their closed life
spans.

Briefly each of us is held in the memories of those
who knew us, who were contemporary with us in life.
Somewhat longer we are remembered if we attain some
fame. We are recalled *as others perceived us*, not as we
knew ourselves. But at any rate, our personal effect,
particular quirks of personality, private and public
deeds, persist in those memories. For a while we may
be brought to the eye and ear by photographs, video-
tapes, family anecdotes passed to perhaps a third

generation beyond us. After that, we become opaque: a name in a genealogy, or in legal documents stored on some back shelf...names with dates, inscribed on gravestones.

Paleontologists and archaeologists learn a great deal from fossil remains—a vanished one's physical structure. They can know whether malnutrition, arthritis, accident or even murder assailed that bony frame. But the soft tissue of experienced consciousness eludes their investigation.

What might be learned from *my* bones, should some future archaeologist uncover them? A woman perhaps, discovers me...her sable whisk unveils my shin, my pelvic girdle, from deep loam. What oracle would my ribs whisper? My vertebrae lie disarticulate. Her fingers find the lump on my right foot's metatarsus where a fracture knit after my marathon. There are my teeth, still intact within the jaw, even the wisdoms crowned with gold. Yet what of missing parts? No flesh endures to tell of the womb's removal—that scar was in soft tissue. No orbit gapes in mid-brow to declare the blow at psyche's center, when a third eye opened after loss of love.

Bones leave unmapped my joys and anxieties: the teen-aged girl running for the sheer fun of it through meadow grass; the woman of forty-five years trotting through her marathon, each step knitting up rents in self-esteem that a ruptured marriage had inflicted. My skeleton will not chronicle the bedtime stories shared with son and daughter, snuggled next to me, nor the painful separation from that beloved daughter when she fled to far Taiwan, seeking foreign culture to heal her loss of father.

Whether from Olduvai Gorge, a Tennessee burial mound, or ancient family plot, our remains decanted from earth's dark ark are mysteries only half-revealed.

Yet once I was present at an electric connection with the reality of a long-gone being.

Ned Swigart was in charge of an excavation of early woodland culture in Washington, Connecticut. Ned founded the American Indian Archaeological Institute. The day I visited, several teenagers were working with his team at an advanced dig. A framed screen had been set up. All earth material was passed through it, to catch any fragments of artifacts that might have been missed. Some sections of the rectangular pit had been dug down six feet. Here in cross-section lay the multi-colored bands of time's strata.

This was not a site wherein fixed habitation was known to have occurred, and certainly was not a burial ground. It was a location believed to have been used for temporary encampments. Procedural rules prohibited dislodging any embedded object until Ned or a senior assistant had photographed it *in situ*.

There was an exclamation from one of the youngsters. He had uncovered a worked stone. We flocked to the margin of his ditch. Ned whistled softly and ran to fetch his camera. After taking photos, he coached the lad through a careful removal of the clay-like soil in which the implement lodged. At last it lay exposed, resting on a small pedestal of earth uncut beneath it.

"Now, pick it up, Tony."

The boy put his hand upon the oblong piece and as he lifted it, shifted it within his fingers for a secure grip.

"Hold it out for us to see."

27

The hefty stone was fully the size of Tony's hand. Its clearly struck, blade-like edge extended beyond his fingertips.

"Tony, yours is the first hand to touch this fleshing tool since an early American let it drop, two thousand years ago. He or she held this hand axe to chop meat from bone. There was probably a hunting party camped here. Do you feel how comfortably it fits your grip, *how you've unconsciously closed your thumb right into that dent there, where its first user's thumb went?*"

Time had drawn its net, like a purse seine around us. We felt the spectral past made tangible.

# BIRDING

I admit it; I'm a "life list" keeper. Right from the start, identifying new species and adding these acquaintances to a growing list of remembered birds was a large part of the pleasure I found when going afield. Fortunately this recreation matured into a richer experience than simply "collecting" birds. Curiosity grew about the behaviors I was observing: migration, territoriality, and predator/prey strategies. At mid-life, I returned to school and put an academic foundation under the twenty years of field experience I had been accumulating.

It was after I married, and was carrying our first child under my heart, that I slung a pair of binoculars around my neck and began to discover the avian community that shared living space with my own species in exurban Newtown, Connecticut. In the initial year, novice though I was, I came to recognize over seventy species of birds within strolling distance of Main Street. Delightful acquaintances: Goldfinch, Oriole, Scarlet Tanager, Blue-winged Warbler, Rose-breasted Grosbeak. In a near-by woodland, I learned the Great Crested Flycatcher's *brrreep!* and the Ovenbird's ringing cry; heard the difference between a Flicker's whicker and the whinny of a Pileated Woodpecker. This recreation grew into a satisfying obsession. There may be a gene or two coding for pack rat in my personality, for no rodent collector of baubles ever experienced more acquisitive pleasure than I as my life list enlarged!

Soon as possible, I took my two pre-school youngsters along when birding. Into the back of our old Ford station wagon I packed them. Mothering two children wasn't going to keep me housebound! Debby and Chuck learned early the salient fieldmarks of songbirds and waterfowl. Their vocabulary was well-larded with *eye-brow stripe, spotted breast, yellow rump,* and *wing-bar.* When they were older, I must confess we played hooky from school should a May morning be alive with waves of migrant warblers. My truant young ones and I found our classroom in the thickets and fields.

In winter, we went to the Housatonic River—a stretch of it that flowed below the Shepaug Dam. Here strong currents kept water ice-free. Black Ducks—dusky birds with silvery underwings—flew over us. We counted flotillas of elegant Common Mergansers—racy, streamlined bodies and thin carmine beaks well-suited to their fish-eating habits. We laughed at the chubby Golden-eye drakes tossing their heads back upon their shoulders in courtship displays.

Here also, we saw Bald Eagles. They wintered along this part of the river because injured fish, the worse for wear after passing through turbines of the hydroelectric dam, provided them easy breakfasts. The eagles arrived mid-December and stayed until mid-March. Initially we found four to six eagles present,

# BIRDING

but as the 1960's progressed, fewer birds appeared until only a single adult showed up in 1970—indication of the catastrophic decline in Bald Eagle populations due to DDT's lethal effects. After aerial spraying and other uses of this chemical were banned, fish-eating raptors made an excellent recovery. The natural world is resilient if given half a chance. By 1980, eight eagles again patrolled the river, and at the decade's end, as many as twenty were wintering in the dam's vicinity. How fine it is to see these great birds playing again in our Connecticut sky!

## FEBRUARY EAGLE

I watched you play
in air over the river,
mock-stooping on ducks,
broad-winged, row upward
clear the ridge, start soaring.
Your primaries, slotted,
let sky through feathered quills.
The Immelmann turn you threw
across blue,
half loop then roll,
up-ended the valley and I standing in it
felt vertigo.
I lost you when you coasted a thermal
into high distance
but you kept a fix on me.
At the peak of your tower,
folded elbows became one delta wing
hurtling down a long curve,
function of power,
leaving your feminine scream
behind in the zenith.

As our children matured, we took them on holiday visits to wildlife refuges. Our family favorite was Chincoteague—on the DelMarVa peninsula. Here we saw thousands of Snow Geese, Tundra Swans, a dozen species of ducks, and even out-of-place rarities like the single White Pelican we discovered there one Christmas.

We experienced delightful moments in those sanctuaries: the frolic of four otters—energetic quartet of supple bodies braiding; tidal pools along a rocky beach on the Olympic Peninsula, in which large anemones softly waved their pale green tentacles and closed upon one's hand like a velvet glove; a tule marsh in evenglow, over which Short-eared Owls quartered like large, ghostly moths.

Behaviors exhibited by birds fascinated me. Each spring, over a thirteen-year period, I logged the arrival of warbler species as they returned from tropic winter ranges to my western Connecticut home town. Daily, from early April until late May, I canvassed thickets, stream margins, and woodlands for these colorful *Parulids*. Although I was innocent of any academic intention at that time, my data later provided the foundation for a Masters Degree.

Migration is not a random journeying; it is intentional toward specific end-point locations and often is cyclical. For North American birds, the cycle is seasonal: northward in spring, south at summer's end. Elsewhere, avian migration may be keyed to other environmental factors such as wet and dry seasons.

One mechanism that prepares birds for migration is a changing photoperiod—the length of daylight in each 24-hour day. A marvelous cascade of events inside the body is set in motion as photoperiods lengthen after the December solstice. One might say North American birds experience the first days of their *biological* spring in late December. As increasing exposure to daylight changes the hormone state of their bodies, an internal "sexual spring" matures well ahead of our calendar's vernal months.

The avian hypothalamus is photo-sensitive. As it receives stimulus from longer periods of light, it releases hormones targeted for the anterior pituitary. This gland is then stimulated to release hormones that activate the reproductive organs: testes in males, ovaries in females. These in turn produce their own hormones—testosterone, estrogen and progesterone. Rising titers of these "sex" hormones in the bloodstream bring birds into "breeding condition." Without this hormone cascade, a bird literally cannot produce eggs or sperm. In a number of species—those which have migrated elsewhere for the winter—the urge to return to their breeding ranges now grows compelling.

Some impressive feats of physical energy occur in migration. Each autumn, Bar-headed Geese leave Siberia and fly over Himalayan ranges to reach their Indo-China wintering grounds. These birds have been heard honking to each other as they wing over mountains 22,000 feet high. That's more than four miles up! Imagine us endowed with respiration so efficient that we could sing while beating our arms at that altitude!

Many species journey thousands of miles on their annual round trips. How do they navigate? Several factors are involved: topography, celestial compass, electromagnetism, and possibly others not yet understood.

# THE BURNING BUSH

We have discovered that "earth songs" play a significant role in avian navigation; many clues to aid orientation are available within the infra-sound range. Birds aloft can hear the ocean's deep voice and sense this "harmony" thinning as the sea shallows upon coastal shelves; they can hear breakers coming onshore. Birds also tune in on the weather—turbulent fronts miles away. They hear the voices of terrestrial animals below: night-traveling rails rarely put down on urban parking lots; they are tolled instead to their proper habitat by the frog choruses of spring wetlands.

Daytime migrants may be informed by physical features of the earth. "Lay of the land" has significance for creatures who lift their gaze beyond horizons. Think how geese, beating high above at forty miles per hour, see the land revealed: ridgelines, river valleys, the curves of bay and lake guide them on. Snow Geese turn to a new compass heading that will take them to their Alaskan breeding grounds, precisely as they pass over one particular peninsula on the west coast of Hudson Bay.

Hawks are diurnal migrants. They require lifting thermals of sun-warmed air to buoy their relatively heavy bodies and grant them altitude without the grave energy expenditure demanded by constant wing beats. Anyone who watches a "kettle" of soaring Broad-winged Hawks spiral upward, until the birds become pepper spots almost beyond binocular range, will appreciate how thermals save them effort and conserve energy. These circling birds mount 3,000 feet or more without a single wing beat. Since they are on their way to Central America from Canada and New England, this conservation of energy is vital. Migrating hawks sight on each other, one kettle following another into those rising air columns. They also orient by landscapes, avoiding those that do not produce thermals, such as extensive bodies of water. Our New England Broad-wings will not cross Long Island Sound, but rather funnel their thousands westerly as they approach the Connecticut coastline, and cross lower New York state, then into New Jersey.

Celestial navigation in birds has been extensively studied. We know that nocturnal migrants "read" the starry heavens as they move along their flyways through the hours and latitudes. Steering by the relationship of constellations to the constant Pole Star (Polaris) requires a time sense in order to be accurate. Birds do possess an ineffable chronometer—the biological clock. Their ability to "tell time" is laid along mysterious and wonderful neural pathways. Gene-coded ages ago and refined through generations of evolution in these species, the biological clock makes possible the corrections in heading that are necessary as the sky's star map alters with the hour of night and the latitude!

Birds of passage hold to true bearings until their journey's end. If blown off course by storm or confused by fog, birds will make the appropriate compass adjustments when the next clear night permits. A Shearwater was transported across the Atlantic by ornithologists to a western hemisphere shore never inhabited by its kind. Nonetheless, after its release the bird found its way back to its native Hebrides!

Shorebirds migrate by day and night. Let us contemplate an epic traveler: the Lesser Golden Plover. This ten-inch bird nests on the Arctic tundra of Alaska and Canada's northwest territories. By late July, young of the year are a-wing and independent. Photoperiods have been shortening since the June solstice. Restlessness stirs the flocks; an urge to be gone is building. Adult Golden Plovers begin migrating, in unhurried fashion, southeastward. By early August, many have reached the Maritime coast of Canada, Labrador and Newfoundland. Just at this time, Crowberry shrubs are bearing fruit rich in carbohydrates. The plovers stuff themselves, adding reserves of fat and storing glycogen in their livers—much as the marathoner "carbohydrate loads" before a run. Then, flock after flock departs. August can be a month of hurricanes. It is not unusual for entire flocks to be destroyed in a great cyclone. Those blown onshore—Cape Cod, Cape May, Hatteras—will huddle on shore-side fields, beaches, even golf courses until the weather allows them to continue.

Let us follow them: it is late afternoon and hundreds of Golden Plover have been astir, preening, making short flights up and down the beach. Dusk approaches and scores rise into the air. More follow. The birds climb to three thousand feet or so and head out over the Atlantic. They fly at forty-five miles per hour, into the oncoming night. Miles offshore, the flock turns south and beats onward, under a canopy of stars. The birds fly through that night, the next day, the next night, the next day, and a third night. Dawn finds them over Venezuela. They have flown a non-stop marathon of sixty hours, all during which those Crowberries were converted into flight energy. The plovers lose up to twenty percent of their body weight, yet live! They have navigated by star and sun compass over a distance of 2,400 miles.

# BIRDING

The flocks rest on Venezuela's inland savanna (the *llanos*) where they regain weight and restore plumage. Then many will push on to the pampas of Argentina. Here, at the lower end of the southern hemisphere, in a habitat that replicates the openness of their tundra starting point, the adult birds are reunited with the juvenile young of that year. These first-time migrants have flown an inland route, quite untutored by any guiding adults, from the Arctic to Argentina!

The entire population of Golden Plovers will migrate north in the spring, over that inland route. During this passage the birds stop to feed along the way in appropriate habitats. The flocks will traverse South America and Central America, will pass over our prairie states and the prairie provinces of Canada, and finally will arrive upon their breeding range again, in the high Arctic. This annual round trip describes a grand ellipse of eighteen thousand miles!

When I ran my first and only marathon, in 1978, from Staten Island to Central Park, I trotted twenty-six miles and some yards. I also carbohydrate-loaded before the event, but my menu was pasta instead of crowberries. We runners followed a sky-blue stripe painted down the center of the streets we were to course...the stars and sun and biological clock belonged to other travelers.

# CARPENTER'S WHEEL

A good friend of mine devoted one winter to creating a queen-sized quilt. She chose a pattern called "Carpenter's Wheel." It was lovely to see symmetry emerge from disparate pieces—how the pattern, heaped in a pile of unstitched squares, at first was fragmented yet held entire in the mind of the quilter. Form came into being in the singular fashion that expressed her *intention*.

There is universal evidence of pattern and design in nature, as also there is random event and never-ceasing changefulness.

How often do we attempt to formulate coherent and dependable designs for our lives? And how often do we find that those scenarios, in which we invest our fondest desires, require mending?

Flexibility is an adaptive trait in natural organisms. Being able to roll with the punches and on the positive side, exploit novel opportunities, is likely to promote the continued survival of any species, be it bacterium, bird, or human. Both form and behavior incorporate traits of flexible response and invention. Invention, the antithesis of rigidity, drives evolution. It exists at the gene level and is also expressed by whole organisms interacting with each other and with their environments. It is a trait selected *for* in the winnowing process we call natural selection.

When energy for creative writing seizes me, unlike my quilting friend, I usually have no grand pattern in mind. Half-realized ideas and provocative associations swirl in a mental broth. But as I assemble a poem, design is involved—a selection of imagery, choice of word—and my intention brings the poem forward. Sometimes two perspectives sit simultaneously in my head—the poet and biologist attempting synthesis. The more I understand about process and relationship in nature's world, the more richly my poetic imagination is provisioned. In contrast, the *found* poem, that rarity springing fully expressed from psyche to page, occurs in my experience only when some magical connection lights up between a natural world phenomenon and my personal landscape.

Transience, change, dynamic becoming and exquisite loss, all are found in nature, and all discovered in oneself.

Changefulness did not strike me as particularly awesome when I was a young person. I blush to recall how often I assumed things and events were what they seemed at any given moment. Also taken for granted was the notion I could find an answer to whatever challenge came my way, or at least, with an adequate input of energy and thought, could control the flow of events in my life.

What delightful, youthful assumptions! Made possible by a benevolent childhood, a kind husband, secure economic standing, and no unpleasant surprises until mid-life. Older, hopefully wiser, I see differently now.

The epigraph selected for *Coming to Water* (a collection of my poetry) sums up its thematic intent; the quotation is from Herakleitos: "Upon those who step into the same rivers flow other and yet other waters."

That Greek philosopher of long ago conceived an idea of atom-like units, infinitesimal units of being in constant flux. Of such minute units all substance is composed. It therefore follows that all substance is continually becoming something else. Present inquiry into the arcane world of particle physics has led many scientists to a domain of reality once the habitat of mystics.

Quantum mechanics suggests that individual events are determined *by chance*. The *probability* of a class of events can be calculated, but individual, specific occurrence cannot be predicted. In other words, specific sub-atomic events are random! Since we are agglomerations of particles that are constantly coming and going, think how ephemeral we are, and how inherently random! Yet here is the mystery: we exist in a coherent universe, a cosmos in which cause seems to own a relationship with effect.

Our senses, receiving stimuli from the external world and from within our bodies, seem to have arranged a consensus for interpretation of those "messages." Not only does the organism possess its own cellular and neurological coherence, but interactions between organisms demonstrate a similarity of perception. Without this similarity, we would not see prey leap to escape the predator's rush, would not see each and every silverfish dart for the darkness of baseboard crevices when we turn on the light.

Without predictability at the societal level of existence, we would not have been able to evolve culture, language, government. Communication depends upon sets of rules held in common. A shared ground of expectations, and its enforcement, supports functional society. Our most disturbing outlaw is that individual whom we term sociopathic—a person insensible to the rules within which we behave predictably and thus a person who acts without compunction, and without the restraint of our usual apprehensions.

But return to the original conundrum: existence at sub-atomic level seems random, yet from the atom up, through molecules, cells, organ systems, whole living plant and animal entities, expressions of existence are organized, and consequence follows cause. Even the inanimate is governed thus—solid, unmoving granite holds that same dance of being/unbeing within its atoms, yet will "behave" in predictable fashions when subjected to chemical or physical forces.

Could it be that disparate and in-themselves-random instants of being are like those swatches of colored fabric heaped in the quilter's basket? Might those motes of existence require only that an ineffable *sorting* take place, a sorting that would determine their *likelihood* of occurrence, and thus entrain a pattern? Spontaneity and mutability would then manifest, over time, the elegance of organization.

The Cosmos has no lack of time.

# TOTEM

While visiting Mesa Verde, ancient dwelling place of Anasazi people, I was given a magical connection with a very small bird—across the boundary separating species.

I sat quiet, on a rimrock. Day was ending and the sun had set, yet the evening air was still pellucid.

Swifts flung by me, diving to roost within the shadowing canyon. They *whisssed* past like flights of ghostly arrows. High in the sky, an insistent yet sweet trill drew my attention. Birder's instinct, honed by experience, immediately put a name to the sound: ah, Broad-tailed Hummingbird. Looking up, I could just see the tiny dot swooping and rising in bounding U-shaped swags—its aerial display.

No conscious thought or intent came to mind as my arm rose, and palm up, my hand extended toward that distant mite. Instantly, out of the sky's vault, the hummingbird plummeted to hover, gem-like, just beyond my fingertips. Breeze from its whirring wings tingled my fingers. How can it be said? I felt a crystalline *yes*! *Yes* to this wild bird, energetic as an emerald cloud of electrons and I by it transformed, the atom's positive center. *Yes* to impulse, to the gesture without thought, to the instantaneous response. Without need to analyze or scrutinize cause, I *knew* that animal familiar.

It was unlike my usual self to have reached toward that bird. Did it call me forth? We met at a critical juncture—my orderly world had recently gone nova. I had learned that my husband of twenty-one years was involved with another woman and intended to marry her. He had left our home on New Year's Day, eighteen months before this moment on Mesa Verde's verge. Since then, he had occasionally visited us. Afterward, when his lean, red Datsun Z had left our houseside, our daughter would collapse on my shoulder—her tears the wake he left behind.

Our two children were in college. When they came home for the December holiday their father joined us on Christmas Day: beneath the epidermal pleasantries of rib-roast and gifts signed *love*, our children felt a bearing bone dragging from its socket. We kept our conversation light, even a touch jocular, so he would come again, but behind our eyes, earlier celebrations were slipping over precipices. He had shied into a poppy field and shed the winter pelt of marriage. We could not hold him.

It was particularly excruciating that I had not perceived his growing alienation until he finally admitted it. I still loved him, and agonized over the "what-ifs." What if he had let me know his bond with me was slipping, before he took himself beyond a point of no return? What if I'd earlier understood his subtle changes in behavior, growing disaffection? Could we have saved our marriage?

I had felt happy and secure during two decades as wife and mother. My husband was a successful attorney. We both set ourselves high standards of responsibility. Our parenting values were alike. We seemed akin in recreational tastes. However, it was usually left to me to instigate our family adventures. I'd say: "What would you like to do?" He'd answer: " 'I don't know, Marty...what do *you* want to do?'" I'd step forward into the space he ceded. Our vacations were filled with travel: golfing in Scotland, bird-watching both in the States and abroad. Often the children were with us.

Alike in our ethics and in our play, we seemed the perfect couple. There was, however, a significant difference: temperament. I am declarative. He is a very private person. I volunteered opinions and feelings easily, sometimes more emphatically than was comfortable for my husband. I seldom let any sleeping dogs lie. The significance of this only gradually became apparent. It is much clearer with hindsight, after long separation from the pair bond that had muted our dissimilarity.

I used to line up manuscripts on my office shelves with their edges conformed. I kept bathroom chrome wiped clean of spatters, and the stove as well. Therefore, in the first distressed year of living alone, it was characteristic that I embarked on a set of regimes that called upon self-discipline: I enrolled in a Masters Degree program in biology, and raised daily jogging (an activity that had been shared with my mate) into the realm of marathon preparation.

Slowly confidence returned. Trotting forty to fifty

miles each week made me more fit and trim than at any time since my teens. I discovered stamina and endurance undreamed of. To the rhythmic pad of footfalls in an easy gait, my mind could slip its bondage of anxiety and clarify its landscape. I was running an *orderly course*, well-planned.

Pursuing advanced education offered deeper understanding of the dynamic relationships between organisms, the elegant fine-tuning of species' evolution, and fascinating strategies in animal behavior. I went toward my Masters, step by step, under control—I was still wiping chrome!

Yet something else was happening; I had resumed writing poetry, not done since undergraduate years, and I was testing rules never questioned earlier. I was travelling alone, for the first time responsible solely to myself. I felt a mix of ardency wedded to a continuing need for order and control.

What occurred at that moment on the rimrock, with scintillation, wild and spontaneous, humming at my fingertips? My contradictions precipitated into joyful harmony, a harmony not sedate and mellow, but sparking and risky. I saw that I could choose ambiguity and transformation as positive conditions rather than feared ones.

This was vision as an aborigine might know it on his walkabout; as native Americans, trekking their dream quests, would have encountered it. Informing spirit flew to me as a hummingbird. *It could not have come until first I reached toward it.*

We call ourselves the sapient species—brainy and reasoning. However, how powerfully our rational brain assents to magic as well as logic! Through all our cultures we seem to yearn toward the mystery of spirit made tangible.

Early bone carvings attest that something was stirring, when utilitarian handicraft began to include another, more numinous purpose—expressive adornment. Venuses shaped to exaggerate fecundity were mute prayers for materialization of that grace in the lives of those who made them. Art flowered on cavern walls, not as an exercise in doodling, but as representation imbued with passion and spiritual significance. Its very rendering perhaps took place in the midst of rites—spears fixed true in the vitals of an auroch as the stag-headed shaman danced. Stone Age hunters must have felt a visceral connection with the beasts upon whom they depended for life or feared as threats to it.

Totems are created personae believed to inhabit animals or other natural world entities, but their magic lies in the vital *relationship* between these "others" and ourselves. Totems may incarnate or confer powers, communicate special insights, or serve as demons invested with our own hungers and anger. The clan choosing Bear as its kinsman hopes awesome bear nature will become available to its people.

In his solitary vision quest, a boy-about-to-be-man journeys into wilderness. Unaided and undistracted by companions, the lad sharpens all his senses upon the whetstone of the natural world. He hopes to encounter some informing power in a tangible manifestation. If this is granted, he will take possession of and be possessed by this informant. He may assume the name of his kin creature:

# TOTEM

## Takes-His-Eagle

Lean-thighed, in first year of puberty
this spring, you watched the eagles pair,
tossing sticks to each other, in air
the female turning on her back
to be mated.
Talons clenched on talons,
the two as one tumbled.

You found their nest ledge
by the whitewash fall below it.
All summer you crouched in talus
and learned their hunting ground.
Now you dig the pit,
weave a juniper mat
to mask you kneeling in it.
Your hare, live-snared, still kicks
on its staked thong.
Below the lid of branches
hour and hour you wait
for the rush, the thud, the squeal.

And when you thrust your arms
through juniper and grasp
those hard, scaled legs
above their taloned feet,
your clutching fingers jerked, wrenched,
as the bird bursts to fly,
as its furious screech shrills above you,
its wild heart enters you
beating your name.

# THE BURNING BUSH

I am not known as "Broad-tailed Hummingbird," nor is there a totem pole with hummer rampant at my doorway. Yet in my home, over the years since Mesa Verde, hummingbirds have taken up residence: one stained glass beauty suspends in the west-facing window through which light plays as I write; another is depicted in a painting given me by a dear friend; there is a third of crystal within the bower of my Christmas Cactus. Around my neck, a chain with a small silver plaque: the bird engraved thereon hovers silent but steadfast, at a lily's lip.

# DEEPER INTO THE FOREST

Passing into the middle-wood of my fifties, with children grown and twenty-year marriage ended, I needed to re-focus my life. Uncommitted time and energy washed through my days like the idle slop of water in a basin tipped this way and that.

There is a geriatric care facility in my community— Ashlar. Its nursing and custodial staff labor devotedly, providing care and comfort to the residents. I offered myself to the Recreational Department and was taken on as a volunteer "visiting daughter." I little realized how this engagement would hone to a sharp edge my blurred notions of mortality.

Nothing in my life had approached the dimension of loneliness these aging persons were experiencing.

PERSIS: her nearest relative, a son, lives in Vermont. He sends her a can of maple syrup each spring. He is a good son; he writes monthly to his mother. He labors from sunrise to dusk as a dairyman, yet manages to visit every other month. Her other relatives—grown grandchildren and an estranged daughter—ignore her.

JOSEPHINE: a welter of kin lives within forty

miles, yet none can visit her because she is so furious at being "installed in this home" that she refuses to see any of them.

ALICE: her sixty-eight-year-old son is bedridden with severe emphysema. She worries to tears about him. Nieces and nephews, a couple of grandchildren and even one adult great granddaughter all live within an hour's drive, yet only one compassionate niece visits regularly. The others make their gestures of affection when they join Alice at the annual Christmas and Easter dinners that Ashlar holds for the families.

Time and again these women share their histories with me: they have managed farm and household; coped with emergencies before EMS, 911, and mobile trauma units; preserved foods grown in their own gardens; scrubbed overalls on a corrugated board and hung clothes on lines to dry. These women were sturdy and bore large families. They were burdened, yet knew their competence.

Now they fold each morning into wheelchairs. Meals on their trays never match the flavors describing them on mimeographed menus: *Chicken Creole* is catsup on a wing and thigh. Their nightly hope: may the kind aide on duty answer my light quickly when I must empty my bladder.

Persis is losing her eyesight. She knits endlessly with thick yarn and oversize needles, making pot holders for the holiday sale. She tells me of exquisite crocheted tablecloths she made for her son's wife. She describes a hand-stitched bridal veil she fashioned for her daughter (in happier times), recalling its rich fall of embroidered lilies and lace. Now she dreads her advancing blindness: "It's going to be like manhole covers, closed black lids with me underneath."

Alice has pinned to a corkboard hung on her pastel wall an array of faded sepia prints—photographs taken almost seventy years ago. One depicts a white clapboard farmhouse with a gracious verandah, the home of her married years. She stands in that yard, a slender, upright woman holding the bridle of an agreeable cart horse. Alice recalls that she earned "pin money" each summer by selling flats of marigolds and zinnias she cultivated. She would deliver a number each year to Yale University, only a twenty minute trot down Whitney Avenue.

When I first met Alice, she was eighty-seven years old. She was then strong enough to manage with a cane or could walk behind her wheelchair, using it as a rolling support. She would go out of doors on each fair day, and in season she enjoyed tidying the flower boxes that edged a sitting patio.

Now she is ninety-five. Dizzy much of the time, she has fallen more than once. She is confined by a torso strap to a "geri-chair"—a heavy, upholstered conveyance that cannot be wheeled by its occupant. She sits through her days, legs elevated and wrapped. She has not worn her wide-brimmed straw sunhat in three years; her gardening gloves are somewhere... each night she prays to be spared waking next morning.

I've drawn nearer to them in this decade, these elders. The veil of my relative youth, which screens from me my future self, has been thinning, becoming transparent. There is creaking in my knees when I rise from bed. Yanking the persistent goldenrod from my flowerbed leaves my right arm aching the day after. I find myself getting out of my car to help a paraplegic who is inching his wheelchair across a shopping mall lot. I offer my arm to grandmas at revolving doors. Am I building levees against the future? Good deeds to woo a kind fate toward me? Do I dread a day I may wait for *my* daughter to bring me some gift of the season on her quarterly visit, while doing her best not to fidget, her footsteps hurrying later, away down the hall?

Each year I've walked through woodland seasons: listened to the Barred Owl's January hoot, *whoo cooks for you-hooo*; touched the nappy curls of newborn fiddlehead ferns; looked for Bloodroot's spring petals, yet understood the beak-faced, baleful turtle who rises from his den of algae toward the bellies of goslings. Summer swallows fling their graceful angles through the air but come September will swarm a-twitter to be gone. Leaves fall, glory staining brown, yet ever, under March snow and frozen soil, bulbs will force their new blades sunward and April woodlots will again haze green.

The grace-filled continuum in nature cycles through its individual life spans yet ever restores. This has sustained me in past times of troubled spirit. Will its solace abide should I be bound some day to a wheelchair, and my life confined within four walls?

After my hours with Persis, Josephine, and Alice, I return home to an empty house, cook my solitary dinner, compose myself for sleep. I seem to slip into a forest, where a shadowed presence waits with extended arm. How take the closed hand not yet revealing its script for me, the fist of my own aging?

As in a dream, I revisit a trail I once walked, in an Australian rain forest. The mysterious power of its archaic flora closes around me. Here, on the forest floor, the shadowed atmosphere is like a green sea bottom. Along the trail, eucalyptus rise clean and silvery. Their bark is smooth as skin. By contrast, the fig trees also growing here are roped and shaggy. Their buttresses anchor to earth with huge woody fins, like whales sounding into the ground.

What is this massive bulk coming into view where the trail turns left? A gleaming, tremendous trunk, its wood satiny and cinnamon-red; no, a color more profound—the rust of winter sunset's last, oldest light. Up the tree towers, solid and without fissure. Its bole is so immense, I cannot encompass it by six spans of my outstretched arms as I tiptoe around it. This tree must be ancient beyond millenia. Its spare-leafed branches reach high to mingle with younger neighbors. Smooth burls bulge here and there on the mighty torso, like flexed muscle. I am drawn to touch them, lay my cheek against the beautiful wood...this trunk of time, fastened steadfast into the planet.

Face pressed to living solidity, I feel vision, serenity and prayer arise: when in some unknown future, I lie perhaps impaired or helpless near my death, may I recall this wonderful Mahogany. May I understand it still abides at that blessed place to which I came. May it fill me again with its patient immensity, the healing sense of its great calendar of being, enduring before me, enduring beyond, holding now the moment we met.

# JUST DESSERTS

I recall my mother did not endorse my youthful attachment to "just desserts." She did not encourage my outrage when our eighth-grade teacher assessed the whole class a hefty homework assignment, in order to punish three boys among us for their misbehavior. My indignant, "It's not fair! I didn't do anything wrong!" drew Mother's response that a teacher may do as she sees fit and that her method was intended to cause the rest of the class to censure the unruly boys. Not me! I was mad at Miss Kennedy!

When a girl, I craved recognition for accomplishments. Praise coming my way after achievement was sometimes more satisfying than my deed. Good grades were my goal, and earnest good behavior my style, but these were less for advancement of intellect or social grace than for the approval such merit always called forth.

At thirteen, I was sent to Maine for a summer camp experience. Save for a hospital stay when I was six, this was the first time away from my family for longer than an overnight.

Camp Arcadia was located on a lake, as all Maine camps seemed to be. I was assigned to a group of girls designated "Middies," because we were halfway up the ladder toward the eighteen-year-old Counselors. I was a sturdy girl, a moderately competent swimmer.

One afternoon in August, a ferocious squall traveled across our lake. There were lightning strikes over the water and wind bursts of great force. We youngsters huddled with our counselors in the doorway of our lake-front cottage, awed by the wind-torn scene.

All at once, our swimming float—a square, eight-by-eight foot deck—broke free of its mooring and began to drift slowly away downwind, about ten yards offshore. The counselors let out whoops of dismay and raced to the beach, shoved off a rowboat tethered there, and scrambled with the oars.

The raft was sailing steadily down-lake, but also moving obliquely toward a point of land some eighty yards ahead of it. I sprinted along a footpath bordering the shore and arrived at this little spit just as the raft reached it. Wading into the water, I grabbed the hand-grips that swimmers used to haul themselves onto the float's deck. I held on with might and main, for the squall was tugging at the raft.

"I got it! I got it!"

The rowboat of counselors arrived, along with other senior reinforcements who had run after me down the path. These older girls secured the raft.

I felt like Wonder Woman, my comic book heroine. Surely praise and admiration were going to shower upon me. Not so!

"You should have stayed in the cabin with the other little girls! Let people in charge do their job. Go get into some dry clothes!"

The counselor who chastised me was called

"Bubbles." She happened to be in charge of the sextet of girls of which I was a member. I masked my resentment of her words. She was, after all, the authority.

On August 8, my birthday, a luscious marble cake arrived in the mail. Mother had baked this favorite dessert for me. I shared the large bundt-shaped goodie with my five cabin-mates. There was still a generous wedge left in the tin after we had feasted. I looked forward to finishing it off, following my riding lesson that afternoon.

When I returned to our room at four, I came upon this scene: "Bubbles" and a sister counselor were just licking the last crumbs from their fingers! In a heedless fury, I shouted accusations and outrage at both of them. "How *dare* you help yourself to *my* cake!" was the mildest of my outcries. All campers within earshot were aware of this scene. I was so overwhelmed by the high-handed usurpation of my property that I burst into furious tears. I was a girl who rarely wept.

Did I receive an apology or any sign of contrition? No! I was privately summoned to the Head-of-Camp that evening and lectured on the virtue of generosity!

This was a primal instance of *unjust* desserts! A sullen peat fire of wrath against "Bubbles" now smoldered in me.

The last week of camp arrived. A canoe picnic was on for our group. "Bubbles" had gotten a lovely coconut cake from the commissary, and she basked in the girls' appreciation as we packed three canoes for our outing. I took the bow position in the canoe bearing "Bubbles" and the cake hamper. We set out. In mid-lake, I capsized our canoe. Oh what a lovely sight—that white cake luminously glissading toward the lake bottom!

Of course, this deed masqueraded as an accident. No way to prove otherwise. I was properly upset and profuse with apologies, as we hauled ourselves aboard the righted canoe. The picnic did take place—a little damp, and dessert-less.

As I grew up, my attachment to the notion of "fairness" diminished, and yet some vestige probably endured, for occasionally in a situation where I or someone I cared for was getting the short end of some stick, I would feel the burn of indignation.

Marriage followed on the heels of college. Soon I was engaged in parenting two lively children. My husband and I shared this pleasure. In many ways he and I were well-matched, but we differed in personality. He was diligent in his practice of law, and a dependable counselor. He invested himself in *pro-bono* good works on many community fronts. He was ambitious for me along these same lines, but my inclination was elsewhere: fostering personal relationships, pursuing an enthusiasm for birdwatching, creating seminars and lectures on animal behavior that I offered for minimal recompense to garden clubs, schools and nature centers. He could not understand why I would turn down an invitation to be Selectwoman in our town, or why I did not seek out an agent and expand my lecture programs to a "serious" dimension.

For a six year term, however, I was a member and then Chairwoman of our municipal Conservation Commission. At this time, I was instrumental in saving a 790-acre forest from development. "This will be the thing that gets you into heaven," declared my spouse.

Our children had reached their late teens and

were in college, when, with no advance signals of alienation, my husband left the marriage. I was then in my mid-forties. Interestingly, I never felt this bolt-from-the-blue had anything to do with fairness or justice. The shock and sorrow I felt went far beyond any dimension of indignation.

He and I had taken up jogging in those last years together, and now I continued to jog daily. It had a calming effect upon the chaotic swirl of thought and emotion. Soon I met other runners and began new friendships. A group of us started training for longer distances, and eventually we prepared for a marathon. Unsuspected strength accrued with those miles.

During this period, Mother was a best friend. She too was managing without a mate. She had been widowed early; when Dad died, she was forty-seven. Her second marriage proved disappointing, and I had championed her at the time of her divorce. Now she supported me in my adjustment to life as a single woman. She enlisted as an ally to my marathon training. She would stash orange juice at points along my jogging routes; sometimes she waited in her yellow Volvo wagon, far out on the route, to give her daughter an encouraging word.

By October 1978, I was ready for the New York City Marathon. I trotted from Staten Island to Central Park. This feat was an epiphany, a personal achievement of preparation and endurance. I discovered what I was made of, unrelated to what others thought of me, and it was *enough*. During those four hours of footfalls on pavement, I purely experienced myself.

Mother was there at the finish line. She celebrated my joy.

Throughout Mother's sixties and well into her seventies, we were chums. We often walked together, sharing our mutual love of the natural world. I admired her painting, she enjoyed my writing colleagues and our readings. An accomplished artist, Mother exhibited her work. I saw mine published. We were peers.

As Mother approached eighty, our relationship began to change. The taint of ill-humor was subtle at first. She would ask my help with some matter or other and then shoot peevish rejections at the solutions I came up with. She began to find fault with me—from the way I gestured "too largely" with my hands and spoke "too loudly" in public, to my choice of recreation. If I took off now for a distant rain forest, Mother found all sorts of hazards I should expect to stand in the way of my enjoyment of the adventure.

As her physical prowess lessened, Mother ex- pressed increasing resentment of activities I still enjoyed. As they were no longer options for her, she seemed jealous.

Mother's hip arthritis became severe. She was compelled to use a cane and could not climb stairs—a maddening situation in her two-story, early-American farmhouse. A heart condition now required medica- tion, and Mother hated taking pills. Although her hearing deteriorated to significant deafness, she refused hearing aids. Her obstinate resistance to these "tools" that would have restored a range of sensory competence seemed simple "cussedness" to me; I could not understand why she would prefer to be limited when she had the means to choose otherwise.

*     *     *

# THE BURNING BUSH

## *Journal, 2000*

Now in her late eighties, my mother's animosity toward me is chronic and unmistakable. It seems to underlie even our good hours together. Her anger springs up at the slightest cause. She complains about the junk mail that comes daily, yet opposes my suggestion to simply discard those envelopes unopened. My proposal that she keep a running balance in her checkbook to prevent inadvertent double payments and overdrafts is met with testy rejection. I had to rescue her from cancellation after I discovered a two-month lapse in her health insurance payments, and have urged her to switch to one annual premium payment. She denies any difficulty in remembering and asserts, "There is no need to change my way of doing things!" Whatever I offer to safeguard her or make her life simpler is angrily disputed. When she does allow my help, she micromanages me to the point of exasperation.

These bouts of hostility have altered the way I feel toward my mother. They erode my affection. Every fond time seems to turn into an unfriendly encounter. I've become defensive and hair-triggered myself. Mixed with this is guilt. I am ever aware that someday Mother will no longer be in the world with me. I love her, and this sense of our hours being precious underlies every experience of anger. Once open-hearted, my relationship with Mother has become guarded, and tainted with feelings of being ill-used. Here again, that indignation I'd felt as a child when unfairly treated. My sweet tooth still craves the dessert of justice!

Am I being tutored? Is Mother, all unaware, my rigorous teacher?

She contests her hated aging, clutches to the accustomed prerogatives of a vanished self. I remind her of that younger woman, strong and capable. Her state of waning power is an insubstantial demon she cannot subdue. She casts me as a surrogate antagonist upon whom she vents anger, fear and frustration.

As I receive undeserved slings and arrows, I learn again, in a profound sense, to relinquish just desserts. I am challenged to love patiently and remain an ally of my mother, although she does not recognize me as her ally.

If I manage to hold this larger understanding in mind, I am freed from injured feelings and disappointment. I am freed, as in a marathon, to run the good course of spirit. Stones lie in this course; they will bruise, but I hope I can go the distance.

*May, 2001*

Mother's mind is in disintegration—that really is the word: dis-integration. It wrings my heart to witness this fuzziness expand week upon week—malignant moss—blurring her neural tree.

At Christmas and early in 2001, she could still bring forth any sentence, and contribute her part to easy household conversation. But with spring's budding green, her comprehension began to shed its leaves, leaf by leaf. First a struggle to find her words in narrative, then an effort to find them in dialogue.

And how her temper has changed! The testy, feisty struggle of last year to hold on to authority, and her passionate avowals—"I've still got my marbles!"—are now subsiding into poignant acquiescence, an almost childlike appreciation of her aides and my visits.

Mother is still at home, as she insists she remain. Day and night, professional companions support her safety and well-being there. This disease will drag my mother from the house of her intellect, but she still resides in her "cosmos"—her beloved country home with its gardens, pond, and studio.

That studio: she hobbles to it on the arm of a nurse, to see yet again the score of her paintings hung on its walls, and check whether her modeling clay (cut from the bank of the Seine) is still damp. There on an armature is the unfinished form of a grizzly bear, paw raised to snag a salmon. Mother's eighty-eight year old hands can no longer knead that stiff clay. Still, she sprinkles the hardened form with water to save it from cracking.

Last autumn, I was able to record ninety minutes of her childhood tales, when she could still recollect them and keep on track in their telling. How precious these cassettes will be: her voice, her laughter as she relished her memories.

And when her mind is bereft of coherence, I shall recall many earlier confidences, both sunny and painful, which she shared in decades past. I am filled with those particulars; they delineate my mother.

As she bends, frail, over her cane and winces rising from her chair, I recall she taught a small Lakota Sioux girl *how to skip* so that lame child could keep up with schoolmates running on sound legs. When she will wander in mind from the act of neatly eating a meal set before her, I shall recall how she stitched a pretty bib to catch the helpless drool of that same afflicted child, and thus rescued her from the lunchroom jeers of luckier peers.

### September, 2001

Mother has had a stroke. Her physical and mental condition no longer permits her to live at home. She has a room in a skilled nursing facility in her home-town. She has not lost her speech, and some of the weakness in her left side has abated, but her severe hip arthritis has worsened because she cannot be given anti-inflammatory medication. She can scarcely bear to walk, even supported by aides. She lives in a wheelchair.

My mom and I have been chums, even through the difficult recent years. We've shared a love of the natural world and a perspective-in-common upon our place in that world; we have shared sorrows, laughs, and ironies that have touched our lives.

With pang-filled heart, I now sit in her house and sift carefully the accumulations of my mother's past. It is poignantly evident that Mother herself rummaged through these voluminous materials stored in file cabinets, on bedroom shelves, tucked in drawers and bookcases. I understand now that her anxious insis-tence on "proving" she could manage, and the closed door barring me from her bedroom, were indications of her private awareness that she was slipping. My mind follows the paths her own must have taken as I discover semi-coherent assemblages of the special events and periods of her life: saved letters, diaries, canceled checks, ancient receipts, and pamphlets on subjects ranging from the fine arts to horticulture.

A manila envelope opened reveals the AKC certificates and euthanasia invoices for each of four cherished dogs who lived their spans with our family—those I knew from childhood and her own beloved Simba, the last dog she and my dad knew together.

Here are gathered the menus and dance programs from the *Lusitania*, on which she and Dad embarked for their honeymoon in Europe. Here are her transcripts of 1921-1923, testifying to courses taken in sculpture and construction drawing at the Boston Museum School of Art. Here too is the notice of a scholarship to Fountainbleau; she gave it up, believing it "unfair to accept," since she was engaged to marry. And here is her diary, filled with sketches composed on the last safari she shared with Dad; neither dreamt he had a scant year to live.

Photos, photos: Alcott, Phelps, Adams, Bagg—her antecedents.

And here, her bird lists: the spring arrivals in her garden, the migrant warblers; our *joint* lists naming those we saw on bird walks together.

Perhaps, perhaps, if the doctor can win management over her pain, I may be able to put Mom in my car and take her to the river, one more time, to see the autumn foliage mirrored. Perhaps, perhaps, if she lives to another spring, I may drive her to a certain roadside spot along a woodland stream, and we might hear, yet one more time, the Louisiana Waterthrush's clear-carrying song.

In memoriam
LUCILLE PHELPS LASZLO
January 23, 1913 – January 25, 2002

# Rain forests

## NURSE LOGS

Stilled, they lie—
long green combers
in the benthonic shade
of rain forest floor.
Towering through centuries
into fog-wet air,
these Sitka Spruce and Western Hemlock
built histories—lean years and fat—
tales of themselves remembered
in heartwood's dilations.
Rugged bark, slow to raddle,
resisted borer and fungus,
took lightning's sizzling whip.
Yet even monuments come down
when years enough lay on.
Falling, each opens skylights
calling up new, frail green:
cushion moss, sweet fern, brambles.
Mould and insects soften trunks,
shape mounds of gentled pulp.
Wind drifts detritus down

and in this litter, cones germinate.
Rank upon rank,
young conifers raise the forms
in which they root,
those long, prone swells, inspirited.

*Nurse logs* is a term I encountered when touring with a forester who was interpreting the flora of the Hoh rain forest on the Olympic Peninsula. This appendage off the coast of Washington possesses, on the windward side of its mountains, a magnificent temperate rain forest. The vast majority of its trees are conifers.

Our forester pointed out the supine tree trunks—ancient deadfall—that were scattered about on the forest floor. Many were mantled in emerald moss, like a lush pelt. Growing out of the backs of these forms were rows of juvenile evergreens. Some were small seedlings, not a foot high, and others were vigorous young trees as tall as ourselves. Because they were rooted along the backs of these moldered, fallen trunks, they were arrayed in almost straight rows of growth. It was a moving thing to see a new generation lifting into the space above its root-holds, the very shape and substance of its fostering predecessors.

The amount of rainfall received determines the nature of a rain forest, which may be temperate as well as tropical. Temperate rain forests clothe mountain slopes, or occur in northern latitudes, as does the Hoh forest on the Olympic Peninsula. Tropical rain forests flourish near or at sea level, in the equatorial latitudes.

One cannot explore a tropical rain forest environment without becoming aware of nature's cornucopia of forms. It is a fecund oasis harboring the world's greatest diversity of plants and animals, yet one *hears* more presence than one sees. The secretiveness of this type of forest challenges and fascinates. Patience and perseverance are required to win more than a fleeting look at fauna. One might easily tread upon a snake, camouflaged as leaf litter, or put one's hand upon a sting. It is wise to learn rain forest etiquette: *touch not carelessly.*

Animal populations in a tropical rain forest are layered vertically: critters in the high canopy dwell independent of those on the forest floor and in the mid-realm. They may never meet. Some animals travel through these strata—monkeys are an example—yet the mature rain forest has its own mini-ecosystems, as distinct as the larger ones defined by altitude zones from alpine tundra to sea level.

To gain a sense of vegetative and faunal zoning associated with varying altitude in the neo-tropics, let us glide on imagination's wings down an Andean mountainside.

Just below the treeless heights of the *paramo* is a belt of cloud or elfin forest. It is alive with birds: Conebills, Flowerpiercers, and hummingbirds with names to match their beauty—Glowing Puffleg, Orange-throated Sunangel, Long-tailed Sylph—all easily seen here, as the crowns of blossoming trees are not far above eye-level.

Going down-slope, we pass through the temperate zone. Here robust trees reach high; viewed across a valley's ravine, their canopy resembles massed broccoli heads. Many species of Tanagers, Trogons, Wood-creepers, and interesting raptors make this forest exciting for birders. In this lush habitat, birdwatching is challenging. The dawn chorus of Antpittas, Pihas, Andean Solitaires, and an occasional Bellbird confirms the presence of a multitude, but nary a one to be spied without dedicated application of binoculars to patient eyes, and the judicious use of tape recordings to lure the unseen into view.

As we descend toward the Andean foothills, the transition from temperate to upper subtropic is marked by silver-leafed Cecropia trees gleaming midst the darker foliage. This zone is rich in animals. Primates gambol here. Howler Monkey bands bludgeon the daybreak air with their roars, hurling antiphonal choruses across the woodland acres.

Finally we bottom into a lowland rain forest. This truly tropical zone lies at or near sea level. What a place it is! Save where some trail or roadway is maintained, it is impenetrable. Humid, almost suffocating at times, and hot! Careful skin hygiene is required here; rashes erupt overnight. If one stays within this forest, sunblock lotion is seldom needed, for only bits and slivers of direct sunlight reach the ground. This environment is yeasty with life and rot and life anew. From the tiny carmine frog cupped within his leaf, to the jaguar walking the woodland floor, bearing its dapple on his back, creatures are embraced and nurtured by this world—one can feel its great heart pulse.

Birding tours to these forests have granted me treasured scenes and moments: in Australia, the scarf of Black Cockatoos drifting across the green canopy of an escarpment opposite me, their raucous calls, attenuated by distance, skirling plaintive in a bowl of space; in Brazil, the pairs of Hyacinth Macaws oaring across a sunset sky—male and female matching wing-strokes with scant inches separating their wingtips; in Venezuela, the fraught hours waiting under a nest site at which a juvenile Harpy Eagle screeched to be fed, hoping to see its splendid parent swoop in with a monkey or sloth clutched in its talons—this is the western hemisphere's largest eagle, and would have been a lifetime "best bird." The adult failed to appear, and we had to move on.

Balancing the delightful frustrations that attend birding in tropical forests are the uncommon gifts of magical encounters: the Crimson Topaz Hummingbird gleaming in a splash of sunlight, holding its hover there long enough for generous viewing; the shy and rarely seen White-bellied Antpitta I whistled to a yard from my feet after twenty minutes of patient mimicry. This rotund little bird, with long legs and stubby tail, walked along the woodland floor to me, whistling as it came, peering right and left to discover the other of its kind it believed was calling. I held my breath in motionless joy when it came so near, and it walked on....

The cup is filled; indeed it runs over, as the Psalmist knew.

# YESTERDAY'S RIVER

Amber light floods the African savannah early and late in the day. It reflects in the yellow gaze of the lioness, and ignites fire in the wings of the Little Bee-eater.

In eastern Kenya's Tsavo National Park, the soil is terra cotta in hue. Some animals wear their land's signature: rusty pantaloons sway when the ostrich trots away, and the zebra are dingy-buff rather than the crisp black and white one expects. Elephants bear a sunset stain upon their hides after dusting themselves with this soil.

Even now, the Rift Valley supports generous herds of game. Gazelle browse under noonday's blaze; their tails, incessantly wagging across white rumps, create an impression that the animals are flickering. Roan-red Topi take sentinel stances atop equally rufous termite mounds. Impala, startled into flight, rise and dip and rise again above the tawny grass—a bounding skein of stretched limbs. Giraffe pace in single file through the mid-day mirages. Their legs dematerialize in the watery glimmer of heated air, leaving visions of long necks and knobbed heads, resembling seahorses.

Even with my first immersion in East Africa's

landscapes, I felt an intense affinity for the land and its animals. On our family safari, in 1970, we camped for a week apiece in four enchanting locales: the Masai Mara, the Serengeti, Lake Manyara, and Samburu. At that time, the parks and reserves were not extensively developed. Only one lodge was present in each place. We lived under our own canvas. When we drove out each dawn for our "game runs," we encountered no zebra-striped tour vans. We went alone into the grass, the thorn, the gallery forests. Africa opened her ark to us, and we explored her with joy, wonder and respect.

We returned to Kenya and Tanzania in 1973. Again we traveled independently with our own kit. When one is camping, one hears and sees the intimate, moment-by-moment progression of nature's day.

First light is announced by the Striped King-fisher's trill, followed by raucous turacos shouting their "go-aways." Next arises a chorus of chitters and churrs—rousing tits and starlings. A Bush Shrike's pure bell-note tolls up the sun. We are already on our way to discover what treasure the day holds. When we return, near noon, the air is a-twitter with swallows, flinging their airy angles over our tent peaks.

Doves coo everywhere in Africa. Throaty phrases tell the hours day and night, if the moon is full. And the nights are wonderful. They vibrate to the chesty grunts of hunting lions, and ask fateful questions in the hyena's querulous *whoooop*. Egyptian Geese *shush, shush*, then burst into blaring honks. Has some nightmare raptor just now stooped upon them?

We camped for two weeks in Ruaha National Park. This park was not much visited in 1973. It is remote, reached by a long, perilous drive from Dar-es-

Salaam—perilous because of reckless lorry drivers, using the one highway for cross-country hauls of copper, from mines in the interior. We were nearly killed, twice, by the careening trucks.

Our campsite was on the west bank of the Great Ruaha River. We pulled our vehicles across the stream by makeshift ferry—empty gasoline drums, fastened beneath a plank raft, supported our weight while we hauled a cable to take us across.

Every day, game eddied around us as it went to the river to quench thirst or bathe. There were shaggy Waterbuck and lyre-horned Impala, families of Warthog, and most wonderful, African Elephants!

Cow herds came daily, with calves in tow. The matriarchs negotiated the steep riverbank with care, but their youngsters came down any which way, sometimes headfirst. Elephants strode into the water without hesitation, unlike the antelope, who paused to check for crocodiles before lowering their heads to drink.

Some elephants flopped into the water for muddy baths. Young ones, tooting like tin whistles with excitement, might totally submerge in the roiled river shallows. A few cows always remained on high ground, possibly as look-outs? Occasionally one would rub her backside against a leaning acacia trunk. Might that tree have been pushed off-center by years of contact with elephant buttocks?

One afternoon, we enjoyed an extraordinary interaction with a single elephant. A bull ambled across the sandbars to our side of the river, and stood just below our tents, separated from us by a twelve-foot vertical bank. He plucked at weeds on the undercut slope. With great delicacy, his trunk curled around a plant and drew it out by the roots. He shook it free of sand and conveyed it to his triangular, pink mouth. We were enthralled and wished to keep him there, so we gathered acacia pods from around our camp and poured them down to him from a bucket. His trunk moved like a questing hose as he rummaged through our offerings.

I fetched a leafy branch, jammed it into the cleft of a long stick, and held it out to him. His little eyes, with a strange expression of sagacity, noted the invitation. Up swung his great head, trunk uncurling down its length like the snappers one blows rigid at birthday parties. As he took hold of my branch, I felt a tug of enormous power, and I released the stick immediately. His trunk was a latent weapon. If it struck, it would be a sledgehammer; if it seized, there could be no pulling away. We knelt on the bank-top, beyond his reach, a respectful audience.

Hippo families lived upstream. This is a dangerous animal. If one finds you between its morning graze and the river, he might trample you in his rush to water. A bow wave surges at his blunt launching. Once in the river, he walks the bottom with pinched-closed nostrils but open eyes. He glides buoyant over the churning pistons of his limbs. He may reappear in a quiet circle of ripples—pink-eyed river horse awash in his pool—or may lunge to the surface in an eruption of muddy spray, with his toothed maw agape, issuing bellows from a cavernous gut.

The dawn chorus of birds here at the Great Ruaha ` River was different from that in the Mara. The wild and lovely yelps of Fish Eagles rang at first light. This bird often utters its ecstatic cry while in flight, tossing its snowy head and neck back upon its black and russet shoulders.

Evenings were a bedlam of Guinea Fowl. Flocks rocketed down to the sandbars and took their water ration in an uproar of metallic, staccato voices. Abrupt silences would punctuate this clamor, each hiatus ended by a solo stutter that was prologue to the next flock outburst.

The Great Ruaha River flows in all seasons, both wet and dry. Animals are drawn to it as if they are tributaries called to this generous stream, which like an unfailing artery supports their lives.

There was a "sand river" not a great distance from our camp. This type of stream is filled with water during the wet season, but in the long dry months, water ceases to flow in its bed. Beneath the surface, however, the water lies readily available. Elephants reach it by pawing holes in the sand with their massive feet. Isolated, shallow pools may remain in the streambed as well.

Before dawn, on the last morning of our safari, we drove to our sand river—the Mwagusi—and parked at its bank. We sat quietly atop our roof hatches and awaited what the day would bring.

Mongooses arrived with the first gray light. Hither and yon the active, sinuous creatures scurried, poking their lean faces into every promising hole and crevice.

As a lemony sunrise warmed the sandbars, a troop of baboons came in. Unlike the silent mongooses, these monkeys were a noisy crowd. The fully adult males paced along with tails arched above their bold, declarative buttocks. They were much more robust in body than the others and all the younger males and females glanced repeatedly at these leaders as if keeping informed regarding their movements.

A single female brought up the rear. When she sat down, we saw she had a newborn clinging to her chest. The little one resembled nothing so much as a four-legged spider clasped to her body. A few juvenile females approached the sitting mother and made gestures that seemed to signify they wished to touch the babe. Its mother swiveled away and fended them off. One persisted—perhaps an older sister? The mother continued to shield her infant from the other's paw. Finally this petitioning baboon turned her back to the seated Madonna, and presented her rump. She backed slowly closer, all the while presenting that disarming backside, until she was close enough to stretch her arm between her hind legs and sneak a furtive touch! Then she bounded off.

Large game did not visit the river until mid-morning. When it arrived, it came in an aura of potency and danger. We first noticed a haze of dust appear over the bush beyond the stream's far side. Then we heard crackling branches, the clatter of horn on wood, and chesty, bovine grunts. In another minute, an immense herd of Cape Buffalo poured out of the thicket and flowed down the bank onto the sandy riverbed, like a massive advance of black lava. Perhaps two hundred beasts fanned out to drink from a pool in front of our car. Tick Birds rode their dusty hides and Hammerkop Storks—small, brown, crested storks—foraged midst a melee of legs, snatching insects the buffalo rousted.

Newcomers behind them pushed front ranks of the herd ever closer to us. Suddenly the animals before us became aware we were there. Up swung the massive heads, wide muzzles dripping, the great boss of horn across each brow dark as obsidian. Would they charge, overwhelm us with their numbers? A moment of frozen tension...then with snorts and tossing heads, the ranks wheeled and bucked back through the beasts yet coming behind them. All was uproar. The whole herd turned and plunged in a jumble of galloping bodies, spurting sand and frantic birds. Up the opposite bank the buffalo heaved, crashing back into the thorn scrub whence they had come.

I had forgotten to breathe in those moments. We all found we were gasping after the explosive release of this encounter. We had been in real danger, not through carelessness but because chance had brought us and this mighty herd to the same sand river that morning.

Later in the day, hurrying toward Dar-es-Salaam and our jet trip home, we drove along the lower course of the Great Ruaha River. Where in this river was the water that flowed past our camp yesterday? Had we caught up with it?

Flying back to a Connecticut habitat so different from the one below the clouds, I recalled images of power and beauty: the leopard reclining in leaf dapple, so at one with the sinuous branch upon which it lay that it seemed a Druid spirit there; the great elephant to whom we offered acacia pods, in whose eye resided intelligence near the boundary of our own; and those buffalo—their mass, odor, sound, and energy. We had experienced animals up close, on a parity with ourselves that morning—a serving of wild Africa on that last day in Ruaha National Park.

Our immersion in wilderness, the intimacy of our association with its game, had erased the intellectual preoccupations we had carried with us from the "civilized" world. On the cleansed page of the mind, Africa had imprinted magic.

# THE BURNING BUSH

In mid-life, I returned to school to earn a Masters Degree in Vertebrate Zoology. Before I entered the graduate program, I was required to amass a number of undergraduate credits in sciences I had avoided years before when getting my Bachelor of Arts. Among those courses was one in general chemistry. Its mathematics were a struggle, but many *concepts* later informed my poetry, acting as metaphors. When I learned the chemistry of chlorophyll, I was amazed at how minimal was the boundary between the vegetable and animal kingdoms:

> Leaves unfurled within my veins
> when I first learned
> the properties of chlorophyll:
> carbon, hydrogen, oxygen, nitrogen
> configured 'round a ring
> whose center is magnesium.
> This society summer-dances
> along every twig,
> springs in tussocks,
> lays platters green on ponds
> for frogs to squat upon,
> is harvested by vegetarians

everywhere.
But replace that atom
central to each ring—
magnesium—
with one of iron
and conjure hemoglobin,
that pigment running red
in us.

- The graduate courses I took on the way toward my Masters degree opened windows upon the fascinating mechanisms of evolution. Chemistry had startled me with the discovery that animal and vegetable are not that far apart. Now I came to see that, although animal forms exhibit varying degrees of complexity, there is no hierarchy in the degree of perfection toward which each organism is honed through the evolution of its lineage. It was also delightful to learn that behavior as well as form evolves through the process of *natural selection.*

Novelty in morphology can occur suddenly as a result of gene mutation, yet the new traits will be susceptible to selection's pressure. Attributes are selected for or against, based upon their contribution to the reproductive success of the organism—reproductive fitness—so if seriously maladaptive, the trait will be modified or the lineage carrying it eliminated— winnowed out over time and successive generations.

Changes in expression of form and behavior manifest more rapidly in local populations that have become isolated from the larger, general breeding pool of their species. Evolutionary invention also expresses itself over shorter periods of time in organisms whose generations cycle rapidly. It is not surprising to learn that scientists choose fruit flies for experiments seeking information on genetic changes.

The *adaptive fitness* of an organism refers to its competence in utilizing the resources necessary to sustain its reproductive success—its competence to survive long enough to produce viable new generations. This competence includes ability to evade predation and to hold its own against other species that are competitors with it for the same survival resources—food, breeding sites, etc.

I feel awe and admiration when I observe a creature expressing its exquisite fitness—fine-tuning in form and behavior that has evolved along its genetic lineage until the present moment. Take the Honeybee, for example.

The Honeybee is best served if its foraging behavior operates at top efficiency—think of all those larvae in the hive requiring sustenance! Think of the eggs ever oncoming from the hive queen! It would be costly in time and energy if every day the worker sisters had to search at random for nectar sources. The less random their foraging, the more efficiently they harvest essential nutrition. The behavior that has evolved to meet this need is extraordinary.

"Scout" bees exit the hive early in the day; they canvass the neighborhood for new flowering. When a rewarding nectar source is discovered—let's say a freshly blooming apple tree or field of clover—these scout bees fly directly back to their hive. Then a miracle may be observed: the *bee dance*. These scouts individually execute a little "waggle-run" across a vertical inner wall of the hive. Each bee returns to its starting point and performs its little run again and again along the same path. Other sisters crowd around these messengers (for information is indeed being expressed). Each scout's waggle line transects the wall's vertical face at a certain angle; sister bees read that angle's arc. They also read the intensity (frequency) of waggles in the run. Then they pour out of the hive and, *translating that arc to degrees off the line between the sun and the hive*, fly in an accurate, direct beeline toward the discovered nectar source. They know whether they must fly a great or lesser distance, for the observed frequency of the waggle line has communicated the proximity of the food source.

But you will say the sun's position relative to the hive will alter as the day progresses. Yes it does. However, bees returning to the hive with their harvest, perform *up-dated* runs whose lines transect the vertical in modified degrees of arc. Accuracy maintained!

When I was a youngster, concepts of evolution were illustrated by drawing something like a tree. Lowest branches bore the "simpler" organisms: protozoa, algae, "primitive" invertebrates. As the tree rose upward, it represented ever more "complex" invention: ferns to conifers to flowering plants; mollusks to lobsters to terrestrial invertebrates. The upper tree gave rise to five great vertebrate Classes—the loftiest assigned to Mammals. Although each Class sprouted its assemblage of Orders and Families, the highest mammalian branch was reserved for the Primates, and from this grew apical twigs assigned to the anthropoid apes. This tree's crowning bud was Man.

The past few decades have seen a new theory:

*punctuated equilibrium* has modified the earlier Darwinian view of slow and steady change. This theory envisions periods of stability in life forms along a given branch of evolution, and then sudden (mysterious) spurts of innovation that result in new species. Whatever interpretation may be in vogue, theories will mutate, and new ones emerge!

Being in agreement with current modifications of Darwinian thought, I tell my students about what I call the Bush of Forms—a concept wherein life forms exhibit varying degrees of complexity yet express no hierarchy in the degree of perfection toward which each is honed through the evolution of its lineage.

Instead of seeing the development of creatures over time as a tree, composed of lesser and higher limbs, tapering to an apex of attainment assumed to be ourselves, I ask my students to envision a huge and massy bush composed of a marvelous number of twigs, all of equal attainment. Each twig bears a terminal bud. Each bud is a *perfected* organism, its particular array of adaptive traits in a state of dynamic response to selection's challenges. The dragonfly, the crayfish, the tiger, man, each has reached this moment as fully realized as any other. There is no hierarchy of perfection. Each terminal bud of life's invention is as exquisite as the next.

This is the Bush of Multitudes, the evolutionary bush, burning through its ages with ardency of life, proliferating endless variation in the sweep of time.

On a mountain path, in Africa, I was to encounter that bush.

The preceding chapter recalled privileged days

camping in Africa's great Rift Valley. I had feasted my senses midst the herds and vistas of Kenya's Masai Mara. There it had been easy to imagine we were immersed in the Pleistocene. When I moved on, flying to Arusha, the capital of Tanzania, I experienced a jolt of dislocation as I paused to re-provision for a trek up Mt. Meru. The sensory assault of streets clamorous with vehicles and jostling throngs on narrow sidewalks expunged the gracious perspectives of wilderness. In the bazaar, Masai youths offered bead collars and frail facsimiles of lion spears. Disdain shaped their faces— the hauteur cattle keepers feel toward other tribes. We were white ghosts, carrying no weight.

But now, beyond the city, Meru's forest reaches down, gathering us to calm soft as a fall of feathers. We climb a winding track. Tree limbs wear velour of moss and ferns, and the pale script of lichens. We ascend under the wing-thuds of Hornbills, invisible in the canopy above. Now and again, a Bushbuck slips like a chestnut shuttle through the sylvan coves—coves a fabric of emerald light. The trail grows steep and we labor upward.

At last the amphitheater, long-quiescent crater, filled to its brim with mist. No magma curdles here, but flame-red Poker Flowers candle the turf, turf so rich and moisture-laden that we sink to our ankles in it. Atmosphere beads, lucent, on every leaf and blade. Cowled with silence, this crater. Time pools here.

It is difficult to leave this height, descend to obligations that tick on other clocks. But going down, we meet it—a massive bush a-quiver with birds, shawled in foraging White-eyes:

# THE BURNING BUSH

Here you are, Bush
burning green—
not tree with tapering crown,
no lesser, no superior branches,
you are the massy Bush,
a convocation—
your budded twigs
a choir of budding.
Descending this mountain
I've met you and myself.
Your leaves dance
under a rapture of lime-hued birds.
Form shape-shifts,
every form vertiginous.
And I shiver, pulse under my skin
a vibrato of atoms coming undone
yet coming again—
illusion, yet here.

You are perfector of the moment,
inventor through time, singing,
your green voice singing me.

# ABOUT THE AUTHOR

Polly Brody received a Bachelor of Arts Degree from Mount Holyoke College, and after returning to school in mid-life, earned a Masters Degree in Biology from Southern Connecticut State University. A resident of Southbury, Connecticut, she has traveled widely in Europe, East Africa, Australia and South America. As a biologist and experienced field ornithologist, she lectures on animal behavior and has created seminars on that subject. She has been an active advocate for the environment, and while chairing the Newtown Conservation Commission, she helped preserve 790 acres of prime woodland. Polly Brody is the author of an earlier poetry collection entitled *Other Nations*, has been published in many literary journals, and in 1998 was a finalist in the New Millennium Writings competition. A frequent reader at venues throughout Connecticut, in 1994 she was selected to read at the Aldrich Museum of Contemporary Art and has been a presenting poet in the New England Foundation for the Humanities series, *After Frost: Poetry in New England.*

To order additional copies of
*The Burning Bush*
or other Antrim House titles
contact the publisher at

Antrim House
P.O. Box 111
Tariffville, CT 06081
860-217-0023
www.antrimhousebooks.com
eds@antrimhousebooks.com